MW01537366

Other books in

The Adventures of Anastasia Bucknail

Series

Anastasia and the Fairy Circle

Anastasia and the Catfish Caper

Anastasia and Amal Visit Lady Liberty

Dedication

Anastasia Meets Jackie Robinson is dedicated to the professional baseball players and umpires from the southern Ohio area. Thank you for the entertainment and pride that you have given us. I am confident that there will be others following in your footsteps.

Special Acknowledgment

Thank you, Robert Dafford, for offering your talent to create the impressive Portsmouth Floodwall Murals. Your artwork is a visual tapestry of southern Ohio history and is appreciated by all who have been privileged to see this work in progress.

Special Appreciation

Thank you, Bonnie Sanfillipo, my dear friend. I could not have done this without you. While working together, I have enjoyed raiding your cabinets and giving your dog Louie way too many treats.

The Adventures of Anastasia Bucknail

ANASTASIA MEETS
JACKIE ROBINSON

By

Marina Rae Cheney

Illustrated by Kathryn Rush

©2021 by Marina Rae Cheney

CHAPTER 1

We Found It!

"David, David, I found it! I found it!" yelled Cornel.

Oh no! I thought. I could hear my brothers, Cornel and David, yelling excitedly from their bedroom. I'm still trying to sleep with my precious dog, Buddy, and my brothers have already started their silliness. It's way too early for them to start with all of their nonsense.

Suddenly my bedroom door flies open, and the boys run into my room. They jump on my bed, bouncing up and down, laughing and yelling.

"Anastasia, Cornel found it!" David is yelling as he jumps even higher.

They're using my bed as a trampoline! Buddy bounces off onto the floor, and I'm hanging on for dear life.

"Stop you two! You're gonna hurt my Buddy!" I yelled as I sat up on the edge of my

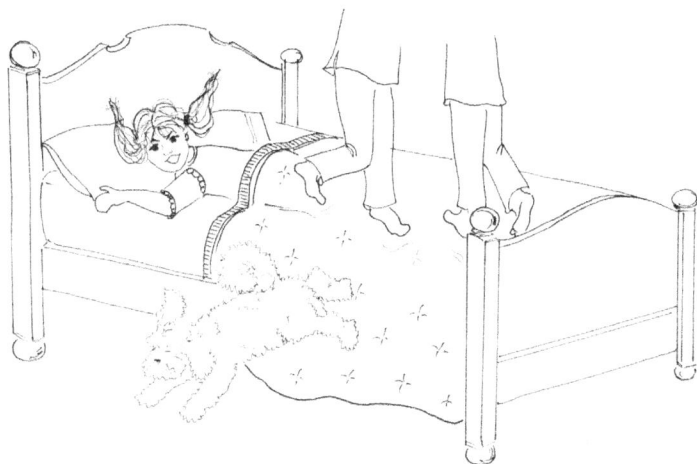

bed. Poor Bud ran under my dresser and looked up wide-eyed at the two crazy boys.

"Ann, you don't understand! I found our Jackie Robinson baseball card that granddaddy gave us!" Cornel yelled. He high-fived David, and they both continued their crazy jumping.

"Of course, I understand! I know who Jackie Robinson is. He was the first African-American baseball player signed to the major leagues. I know a lot about Jackie Robinson and also about baseball."

"Gimme a break Anastasia Bucknail. What could you possibly know? You're a *girrrrrl*." David said sarcastically.

"I know lots!" I insisted. "For instance, I bet you don't know that Jackie's brother won the silver medal when he ran against Jesse Owens in the 1936 Olympics. That was in Germany and, for your information, Germany is in Europe. Ha!"

I jumped off of my bed and continued my speech. "And some more info for you two: Jackie threw right and batted right. And finally, so that you know, Branch Rickey is the man who signed number 42 to the Brooklyn Dodgers. So there!" With that, I stomped my foot on the floor…. just because!

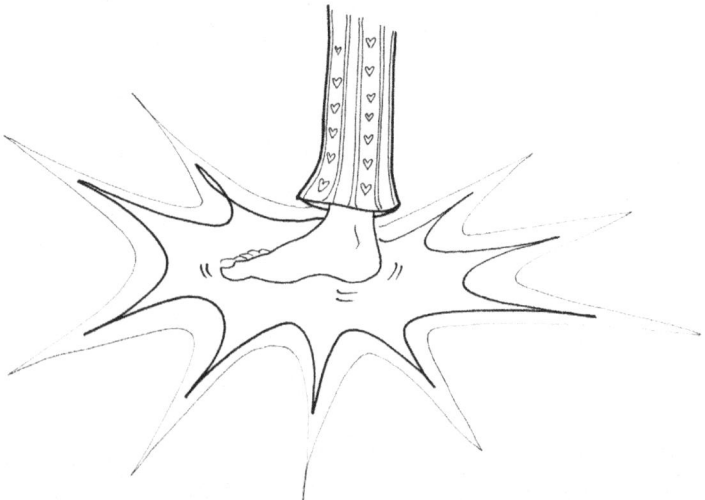

They both stopped jumping and looked at me. "How do you know all this stuff?" asked David, looking surprised.

"Well, for starters, I listen in school when the teacher talks, something you two don't do. Besides, Lou and Granddaddy talk to me about baseball. As a matter of fact, Jackie Robinson is my friend."

When I said that, they both laughed so hard they jumped off my bed with a loud crash. Uh-oh, I'm thinking, Dad heard that.

"Anastasia!" Cornel roared and laughed, "Jackie Robinson isn't even alive anymore! How can he possibly be your friend? You have a crazy imagination. This is right up there with your trip through the fairy circle, and your magic carpet ride to the Statue of Liberty." He and David started laughing and running around my room. I was sure Dad could hear that, and he would be up here.

"Well, I don't care what you think. Jackie Robinson IS my friend! Just ask Buddy."

"Oh sure," Cornel laughs, "Buddy, the talking dog that can even quote Shakespeare."

Cornel rolled his eyes at David, and they both started cracking up.

I grabbed my precious Buddy out from under the dresser and hugged him tightly.

CHAPTER 2

Boys, Get it Together!

Then I heard it. Lou, that's my dad, was coming up the stairs. He was making that sound with his feet that lets you know he's not happy. Lou walked into my bedroom and said, "Ok boys, what's going on in here?"

"Well, Dad, Cornel and David woke me up!" I said. "They are making all kinds of noise because they found their Jackie Robinson baseball card. If you ask me, they need to take better care of all their cards. For one thing, they are worth a lot of money, and for another, they were gifts from you and Granddaddy."

Oh my gosh, I thought, I sound just like my mother.

"You know boys, many times your sister acts more mature than the both of you put together. Now, go clean up your room and get those cards in order."

"We will, Dad, but we're cracking up because Anastasia Bucknail thinks that Buddy can talk and that number 42 is her friend." David chuckled ands rolled his eyes. "That doesn't seem so mature to me," he said.

"Now, don't try to take the light off yourselves. You two were up here making all the racket. Your sister just has a creative imagination. Don't you, honey?"

Dad left my room and walked down the stairs. I turned and stuck my tongue out at the boys. They turned around laughing and ran into

their room. I do love my brothers, but
sometimes they drive me crazy.

"You know, Buddy, I do know a lot about
baseball, and I can play as good as any boy."

Buddy looked at me like he was saying, "I
know you can. You're the best."

I smiled at my angel Buddy and then said, "I
know Buddy, let's clean up the bedroom and

then put on our baseball shirts today." Buddy smiled, and I knew he was excited. We made my bed, hung up my clothes, then everything was neat and tidy as usual.

"Buddy, we are fabulous!" I said proudly. "Just listen to the boys. They're in there pretending like they're cleaning, but we know what they're doing, don't we? They're shoving everything either under their bunk beds or in the dirty clothes basket. Mom will catch them, and then there will be trouble."

"Now, Bud, let's get your Johnny Bench shirt."

Buddy's shirt is fabulous. Granny made it for him, and I love it. It's a light gray T-shirt with red trim and his name on the back. It says **BUDDY BENCH** with the number **5**. It's for Buddy's favorite Cincinnati Reds player, Johnny Bench. He was a famous catcher, and his number was five.

"Buddy, did you know that the Reds won the World Series in 1975 and 1976? Granddaddy says that Johnny Bench could hold five baseballs in one hand. Do you think that's true?"

CHAPTER 3
Lou's Plan

"Miss Ann."

I looked up, and Lou was standing at my door.

"This afternoon, we are going to visit Granddaddy, have supper with him, and then go visit the wonderful murals on the floodwall at the Ohio River. I know we've been there before, but this time I think we will focus on the great baseball players from this area. I think it will be a lot of fun, don't you?"

"I sure do, Dad! Can Buddy go? He's going to wear his Johnny Bench T-shirt, and I'll wear my Jackie Robinson shirt."

"Okay, honey. Get ready, and we'll leave about 3 o'clock. That's 15 hundred hours in military time. I'll tell the boys. I know they'll be excited."

Lou marched out of my room like a soldier.

"Buddy, Lou is so crazy."

"I heard that, Miss Ann. My name is Dad."

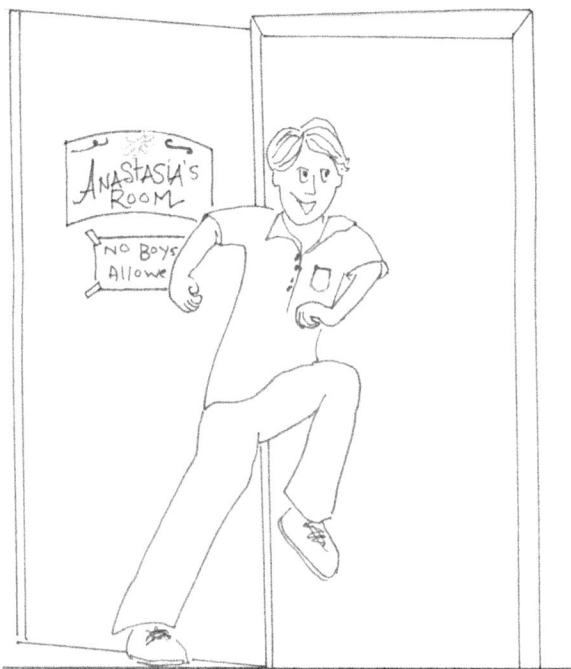

I could hear Lou telling the boys about our afternoon adventure, and they started their rowdiness all over again. I glanced at Buddy and rolled my eyes, "If Lou looks under their beds, Bud, he'll be the one jumping up and down."

"Okay, my little angel, let's get your Buddy Bench shirt on, and then I'll put my Jackie shirt on too. Hold up your little front paws, and I'll slip it over your precious little head. Now, let's comb your ears, and you'll be all set." Buddy has a special comb for dogs, so it doesn't hurt him when I want to make him look extra beautiful. Today is one of those days.

"I know Bud, let's put red bows on your ears to represent the Cincinnati Reds, and I'll put blue bows on my ponytails for the Brooklyn Dodgers and Jackie." I combed Buddy's ears and tied each one with a bright red ribbon into a perfect bow. Next, I brushed my hair into ponytails, one on each side of my head, and tied a dark blue bow on each one.

"We look fabulous, Bud!" I exclaimed. "Okay, now I'll put on my Jackie shirt. See Buddy, it's white with a navy blue **42** on the back. That was Jackie's number. My shirt has **42** also, and it says **ANASTASIA.** Don't you just love it! Granny makes us the coolest things, doesn't she, my precious angel?"

I slipped my shirt carefully over my perfectly placed bows. I picked Buddy up and put him on my dresser so we could look in my mirror together. Buddy stood up on his back

legs and turned around to look over his shoulder and see the back of his baseball shirt. I know he was thinking about how fabulous he looks.

"Bud, we look like twins! Not identical twins, but fraternal twins. We talked about that in school. It has something to do with DNA. I don't remember exactly what the letters stand for, but I do remember that DNA makes us who we are. Fraternal twins don't necessarily look alike. You know Buddy, like my two best friends, Ellie and Luca. They're fraternal twins."

"Anyway, Bud, we look great, and we're ready to go! I'm going to take my baseball glove with me. I'm also going to ask Lou and Granddaddy to start saving baseball cards for me. Granddaddy has lots of great ones."

Just then, I heard Ginny, my mom, call from downstairs. "Kids, when you finish your rooms, I want you to come down here and help me with some chores."

Buddy and I ran down the stairs and into the kitchen. The boys almost tripped over each other, trying to see who could get there the quickest. I know they hate chores, so they probably think they won't have that much to do. I also know they are excited about today's adventure.

CHAPTER 4
Chores

"Mom, what are you cooking?" I questioned. "It smells like your fabulous pasta sauce!"

"Honey, I'm making lasagna to take to Granddaddy's. He loves it, and so do we. He's

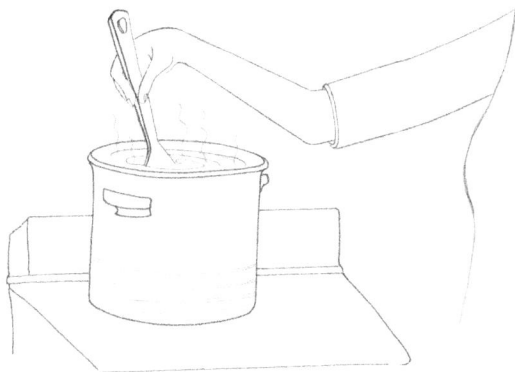

making a salad and garlic bread, and we'll have a nice supper before we go see the murals."

"Okay, here's what we need to do: Miss Ann, please load the dishwasher. Boys, get the clothes out of the dryer and fold them. Do it neatly this time so they won't be all wrinkled.

When you finish with the laundry, take it upstairs in the basket, set it in my bedroom, and then go dig your clothes out from under your beds and put them where they belong."

Cornel and David looked at each other and then looked at Ginny in disbelief.

Ginny smiled and said, "A fairy that lives in our backyard told me. Now hurry and finish

your chores. When your dad finishes cutting the grass, we'll be ready to leave."

"Mom, please don't let Dad mow over the place where the fairy circle was," I pleaded.

"Miss Ann, don't worry, the mushrooms are gone and will probably never return."

"Mom, you never know when it comes to fairies."

"I know," agreed Ginny. "Sometimes strange things do happen."

CHAPTER 5
Let's Get Ready!

"Mom, I am so excited about seeing the murals again, especially the part with the baseball players. And, by the way, I have decided to ask Granddaddy to start saving baseball cards for me too."

"He would love to do that for you," Dad said as he walked into the kitchen. "He has been saving baseball cards for as long as I can remember. As soon as everyone has finished

their chores, we'll leave. Don't forget to take some food for Buddy."

I finished putting dishes in the dishwasher. I could hear the boys upstairs digging their clothes out from under their beds. I smiled.

"Okay, Buddy, let's get your food ready." I poured some of his food into a plastic bowl and snapped on the lid.

I took Buddy outside and we walked over by the big maple tree where the fairy circle used to be.

"I sure wish the mushrooms were still here and that Princess Colleen would come for

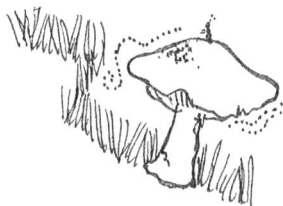

another visit." Buddy looked at me in agreement.

"Buddy, I almost forgot! I want to take my notebook on our trip today to jot down interesting things. Let's go! I'll race you upstairs!"

Buddy and I ran into the house and up the stairs into my room. I grabbed my notebook and hopped back down the stairs. Buddy stayed close behind me.

"Miss Ann, you two look wonderful in your baseball shirts. Don't they, Lou?" Ginny commented.

"You look like professional ballplayers," Lou answered. He patted me on the top of my head.

"Okay, Miss Ann, I think we're all set. The lasagna is ready, and Buddy's food is packed." Mom walked toward the stairs and called up to my brothers, "Boys, we're ready to go."

The boys came flying down into the kitchen, each with his baseball glove. "Mom, we're so excited!" David announced. "We love the baseball murals, especially the one with Jackie Robinson and Branch Rickey. Mom, did you know Anastasia is friends with Jackie Robinson?" David was being 'sarcastic David' again.

Dad walked in, picked up the lasagna carefully, and put it in a carrier because it was still really hot. "Okay, guys, the wagon train is ready to roll," he announced.

Lou says the craziest stuff.

We all climbed into the SUV, and it was a struggle as usual. The boys were noisy and climbing all over each other. I was afraid they

would crush Buddy. Buddy jumped in the front seat with Ginny to save himself. We finally got ourselves together. Dad in the driver seat, Mom in the passenger seat, and the boys and me in the back. Seat belts clicked, and off we went.

A few minutes later, Buddy jumped back to me and rested his little head on my neck. He is so soft and snuggly. We looked out the window at a beautiful sunny day. The tiny dust drifting in the air reminded me of the little crystal sparkles I saw on the day the boys threw Kitten, the catfish, into Dreamland Pool.

"Ann. Ann, we're here." Mom said as she unhooked her seat belt.

I smiled at Mom, hugged my little Buddy, and opened the door. The boys and I climbed out of the SUV and ran around to granddaddy's back porch. Dad and mom followed, bringing the lasagna and Buddy's food.

CHAPTER 6
Dinner with Granddaddy

"My favorite grandchildren!" Granddaddy called as he walked out onto the back porch carrying garlic bread and a large bowl of salad.

"Granddaddy, we are your only grandchildren!" David announced, laughing.

"I know. That's why you three are my favorites!" Granddaddy thinks he's funny, and I do have to admit that sometimes he is.

I put Buddy down by the dish that Granddaddy had already filled with water. I gave him his food, and he started chowing down. The adults were setting the table and talking about adult stuff like the stock market, new roads, and other boring stuff. Money stuff, I guess.

"Okay, kids, let's eat!" Granddaddy said happily as we all took our places around the table.

The food was delicious, and it was beautiful out in the backyard. We were all kind of quiet, including the boys, just enjoying our dinner and the fantastic weather.

After we finished eating, Granddaddy got up and went into the house. He came back a few minutes later and said, "Miss Ann, I have a surprise for you. Now close your eyes."

I love surprises, so I did what he said.

"Now you can open them."

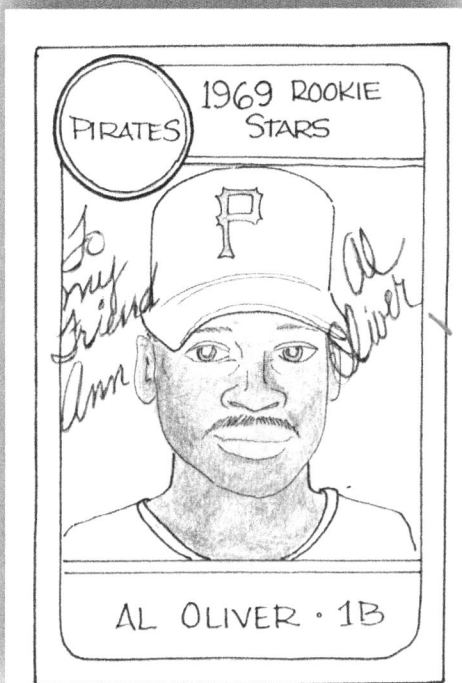

1969 ROOKIE STARS

PIRATES

AL OLIVER · 1B

I looked up and then down at the table. There was Al Oliver's rookie year baseball card looking back at me.

"Oh my gosh! Is this for me?" I looked at Granddaddy, my parents, and my brothers. I jumped up from the table, gave Granddaddy a big bear hug, and danced around holding my perfect precious prize. "I can't believe this! Look! It's even signed! It says *To my friend,*

Ann, Al Oliver. Granddaddy, I can't believe this! Where did you get it? How did you get it? How did you know I wanted to start collecting baseball cards?!"

"Well, first of all, as you all know, Al is from the Portsmouth area. I ran into Al downtown, and I asked him to sign it, and he was kind

enough to do so. Secondly, the fairies that live out back in the sassafras tree told me that you wanted to start a collection." Granddaddy smiled, looked at Dad and winked.

"Thank you so much, Granddaddy!" I turned and looked out at the sassafras tree. The sun was shining down through the fluttering leaves, making them sparkle like diamonds. "Thank you too, wonderful fairies!" I said.

The boys started laughing again, and then David said, "We have one of Al's cards, Granddaddy. Can you ask him to sign it for us, or do we have to ask the fairies first?"

"Now, boys, leave your sister alone. I can pick your card up this week, and I'm sure when I see Al, he'll be glad to sign it for you," Granddaddy assured the boys.

Granddaddy continued, "Here's a little information for you about Al Oliver, so you'll be all set when you see his picture on the mural today. He played ball for years. As a matter of fact, he played outfield and first base for the Pittsburgh Pirates in 1971 when they won the World Series."

Still, in teaching mode, Granddaddy said, "You are going to have a wonderful adventure this evening. Robert Dafford is the artist that created the floodwall murals. I believe he is from Lafayette, Louisiana. He has painted murals all over the world, and we are truly fortunate that he has come to Portsmouth to display his artistic talent."

"Dad, would you like to join us on our little adventure?" Lou questioned.

"No, thank you, son. Someone has to stay here with the fairies."

Everyone smiled.

"Okay, kids, let's go," Ginny said. "Miss Ann, grab Buddy and the plastic container, and you kids thank your grandfather for having us. Dad, I'll leave the rest of the lasagna so you can have it for tomorrow night's dinner. Ann, honey, let me keep your Al Oliver card for you until we get home."

"Okay, Mom," I agreed and handed her my fabulous new baseball card.

"Ginny, thank you for the wonderful lasagna, and you kids have fun." Granddaddy gave us all a big hug.

We thanked Granddaddy and scrambled back to the SUV. We all climbed in, and David reached in the back and got his and Cornel's baseball gloves. I was so excited. The weather was perfect, and the sun was just starting to go down. I was sure this was going to be a magical night.

CHAPTER 7
Cotton Candy Cloud

"Now, kids," Lou said. "It won't take long to get there, so let's go over a couple of things. The amazing detailed images cover the last two centuries and highlight special events, places, periods of time, and well-known people from Portsmouth and the surrounding area. How many years are in a century, kids?" Lou always likes to quiz us.

We all answered at the same time, "One hundred."

"Good job! As I said before, tonight we are going to focus on the baseball players. It's amazing how many talented players are from around here. If we don't have time to discuss them all, we can always make another trip. Can't we, Ginny?"

Mom smiled and nodded.

It was just starting to get dark, and I thought what a beautiful night it would be for a baseball game. I love riding along when Dad is driving.

The purring sound of the engine always makes me feel safe and relaxed. I settled in to enjoy the ride.

All of a sudden, I could smell popcorn and hot dogs and hear a noisy crowd cheering. Is there a ballgame near here? I wondered. I

looked out my window and could see Dad turn onto Front Street, where the murals are. People were walking with their children. Cars were slowly driving by, so their passengers could look out their windows at the beautiful artwork. It was all very exciting.

I then heard a low roar and saw motorcycles driving slowly down the street toward us. As I watched, the motorcycles started to look strange. As they got closer, the smoke that poured out of their tailpipes began to change color. The smoke was pink, yellow, blue, and some brilliant white. It was a rainbow of changing colors. The different colors began floating toward our car, and the sound of the motorcycles' roar turned into the song *Take Me Out to the Ballgame.*

The people walking in front of the murals started cheering and waving pennants just like you would see at a major league baseball game. The colorful cloud of smoke drifted toward us and came through Ginny's window. It curled softly around Mom and Dad, but they continued talking as if nothing was happening. The rainbow of colors glided into the back seat where the boys and I were sitting. It wrapped itself gently around all three of us, but the boys didn't seem to notice. They kept chatting about baseball cards. The beautiful cloud smelled just like cotton candy. I couldn't believe it! The colors moved gently out the window on my side of the SUV and then up toward the mural.

"Ann. Ann. I've been waiting for you."

Where is that voice coming from? I didn't recognize it. It wasn't my brothers or my

parents and not Buddy because his voice isn't that deep. I looked at Ginny and Lou, and they were chatting about something, and the boys were still talking baseball. Am I the only one that heard the voice?

"Ann. Anastasia. I'm up here."

I looked out my window and up at the mural. We were right in front of the Jackie Robinson and Branch Rickey mural, but it looked different. Jackie Robinson was standing up. He was looking down at me and waving. Branch Rickey was still sitting down, but he was also waving at me. Then Jackie started speaking.

CHAPTER 8

Ann or Anastasia?

"Hello Ann. I've been looking forward to your arrival. I know how much you like baseball and that I'm your favorite player, so I have something fun planned for tonight."

This can't be happening! This is not real! I shut my eyes and rubbed them, knowing that when I looked again, everything would be normal. When I opened my eyes, Jackie Robinson was standing right beside my door. I looked up at the mural where he was supposed to be, but the only person I saw was Branch Rickey smiling down at me. Jackie opened my door, and I got out and stood next to him. I stared up at him in amazement.

"So, Ann, first things first, would you prefer that I call you Ann or Anastasia?" Jackie questioned.

I turned around and showed him the back of my shirt. I set Buddy down, and he turned so

Jackie could see the back of his shirt too. Jackie gave me a thumb's up and a big smile.

"Well, then, *Anastasia*, it is. You can call me Jackie. It is such a pleasure to meet you."

"Are you sure that it is all right to call you by your first name?" I questioned. "My granny says I should always call adults by their last name. It's respectful."

"Well, you told your brothers that we are friends and friends call each other by their first names, don't they?"

"They do!" I said with delight.

"Then it's perfectly fine with me," he said kindly.

"Okay, now pick up little Buddy Bench. We're gonna play baseball!" he said with a big smile on his face.

How did he know that I told my brothers that he and I were friends, I wondered?

CHAPTER 9
Baseball Magic Begins

Just then, the colorful cotton candy cloud floated toward us. It wrapped itself around Jackie, Buddy, and me. Our feet left the ground

as the cloud lifted us into the night air. We began to float higher and higher over the floodwall. I was so scared that I shut my eyes and covered Buddy's eyes with my hand. I was afraid that we were going to fall right into the Ohio River.

"You can open your eyes, Anastasia. We're almost there," I heard Jackie say.

I slowly opened my eyes and gazed down in front of us. To my relief, the river was no longer there. Instead, there was a huge baseball field with bright lights shining against the chilly, dark summer night. It looked just like the Cincinnati baseball field that Granddaddy took us to last summer. I could hear the cheer of a crowd and could smell the fabulous baseball stadium food again. I held Buddy close to me and grabbed Jackie's hand. He looked at me and smiled. We floated down to the field and landed near first base.

I put my precious Buddy down, and he turned to us and said, "See you later, guys. I'm playing catch tonight." My little angel trotted toward home plate, looking so proud.

The crowd started yelling, "Go, Buddy! Go, Buddy!" Fans were holding up signs that they had made that said, **WE LOVE BUDDY!** The

cheering was so loud that I had to cover my ears. When Buddy reached the plate, he turned around like a proud little peacock and showed off his Buddy Bench jersey. The roaring started again from the bleachers. My precious little prince is a superstar!

"Well, Anastasia," said Jackie, "I think Buddy has a career in the majors." I looked up, and smiled at him and he chuckled. He then started talking about our lineup.

"You, Anastasia, will play first base. You're a leftie, and they make good first basemen. I'll be your coach. Now check out the pitcher's mound."

I couldn't believe my eyes! There was my mom, Ginny, warming up with Don Gullett, a famous Reds pitcher. He was showing her how to throw a fastball. She threw one directly over home plate, and Buddy made a perfect catch. He turned and bowed to his loving fans and the cheering started all over again. Even though the crowd was screaming and excited about the

game, I could still hear everything Ginny and Don were saying.

"Now Ginny," I could hear Don Gullet say, "Let's see your slider." Ginny got ready and wound up for the pitch.

"Jackie, I don't understand how we can hear them talking over all of this fabulous cheering!"

"Baseball is magical, Anastasia," he said with a grin. "Now check out the entire infield."

To my delight, Lou was playing second base and warming up with Cornel, who was at short. David was at third, and Al Oliver was the third base coach.

"Jackie, we don't have any outfielders," I commented.

"With this terrific group of infielders, I think we'll be just fine," Jackie said with confidence.

I smiled at him and then turned toward Ginny again. She threw a beautiful slider toward home plate. Right before it reached Buddy, something odd happened. The ball changed into one of those juicy slider burgers that you get from Hickie's Hamburger Inn. Everyone knows they're fabulous! Instead of reaching for the ball, Buddy jumped up, opened his mouth, and devoured the juicy treat! Again the crowd went wild and started cheering for Buddy.

CHAPTER 10

What Goes Around Comes Around

The home plate umpire yelled, "PLAY BALL!" The first batter ran out to the plate. He got in position and was ready to swing.

"Oh no, Jackie!"

"What's wrong, Anastasia?"

"That's Sean! He lives down the street from me. He used to tease me all the time when I had braces. He still calls me *brace face!*"

"Well, I know those things can hurt your feelings, but what goes around comes around. Let's see what he can do."

Sean looked over at me and gave me his usual smirk. He got ready and stood in a batter's position to swing. I imagined him knocking it out of the park. Ginny wound up and threw a fastball like a speeding rocket.

"Strike One!" yelled the umpire. Buddy turned and bowed toward his screaming fans holding up the rocket ball in his glove. He turned back around and jetted the ball back to

Ginny. He then started giving her signals. She

nodded and got ready for the pitch. I got low to the ground just in case I had a chance to tag him out at first. Jackie said, "He'll probably hit to left field."

Ginny threw an 'Uncle Charlie.' It was the fastest curveball I'd ever seen! Sean nailed it! Instead of hitting a perfect fly like I thought he would, he slammed a grounder right toward David at third. My brother scooped it up and drilled it straight toward me. My hand felt the sting as the ball made a solid thud in my glove. I bent down and quickly tagged Sean on the leg as he slid toward first base. Sean jumped up and hustled back to the dugout. He didn't even look at me.

He'll never forget this, I thought. I looked up at Jackie.

"Remember what I said, Anastasia, what goes around comes around," he smiled and gave me a high five.

David and Al Oliver were high-fiving. The crowd went wild! I looked up in the stands, and the Portsmouth High School cheerleaders were jumping up and down and cheering, "Go, Anastasia! Go, Anastasia!"

"Batter up!" called the umpire. A new kid ran out to the plate. I didn't know who he was, but he looked really strong. He was a leftie, so

the infield moved to the right. I got down in
position and got ready for the ball. Ginny
wound up and threw a fastball and, of course,
Buddy made a perfect catch.

STRIKE! Signaled the ump with a huge
gesture.

Buddy turned and saluted to his adoring fans
and then threw the ball back to the pitcher, my
mom. I can't believe all of this is happening.

The batter got in position again, and Ginny
threw a great curveball. The batter connected,
and a loud cracking sound ripped through the
stands. It was a perfect hit toward center field.
Cornel turned toward the outfield and took three
of the biggest giant leaps I have ever seen. It

was almost like he was flying. On his next leap he jumped even higher, spun around, and snagged the ball right out of the cool, dark, starry night. How did that happen? That's impossible! No one can do that! I turned and looked at Jackie.

"Jackie, that's impossible!"

He just smiled.

CHAPTER 11
Good Night Jackie Robinson

Suddenly all was quiet. I looked up at the fans, but they weren't there. I turned toward the

infield. It was deserted. Buddy was standing at my feet, pawing my leg for me to pick him up. Once again, the cloud of beautiful colors had wrapped itself around us and was lifting Buddy and me into the cool night air.

I looked down at Jackie.

He waved goodbye and said, "See you soon, friend."

"Ann. Ann honey. Wake up," I could hear my mom say. "While you were sleeping, I wrote down a few interesting things in your notebook about the murals."

I gathered my stuff and crawled slowly out of the SUV. I carried Buddy into the house and up into my bedroom. I was so tired. I put on my pj's and laid down on my bed and cuddled Buddy.

I could hear the boys, still full of energy, talking baseball and going through their cards. They were discussing Jackie Robinson and how they were going to put his card in a special place in the box.

Suddenly, Cornel started yelling, "David, David, look at this!"

"What? Wait, that's impossible!" David said with astonishment. "Another Jackie Robinson rookie card? I don't remember having two."

"David, look! This one is signed! Can you believe this?" Cornel said.

They got really loud and were clearly excited about their discovery.

Then it got quiet.

"Wait a second," Cornel said. "David, look closer. Look at what it says."

I could hear David read it out loud.

"***To Anastasia, Your friend, Jackie Robinson,***" *he read slowly.*

There was a VERY long pause, and then I heard Cornel say, "Oh my gosh David, no way."

I smiled at Buddy. We sat up, and looked out of my window at the crystal night sky.

"Good night, Jackie Robinson," I said with delight.

THE END

Marina Cheney is a retired English teacher with twenty-two years of experience teaching English to new English language learners. Marina was raised in Portsmouth, Ohio. She is a graduate of The Ohio State University.

It is Marina's hope that through the fun-filled Adventures of the Anastasia Bucknail series, children will enjoy the reading experience and will build a life-long love of reading books.

Contact information:
marinaraecheney@gmail.com

Made in the USA
Las Vegas, NV
16 June 2022

50304248R00037